The Green Line

Buy the Bottom of Any Stock Market Correction

2nd Edition

By Tim Morris

Copyright © 2020
All Rights Reserved.
The Green Line ®
ISBN: 9781096125259
Published by ZML Corp LLC

Table of Contents

Disclaimer 3

About the Author 5

Introduction 7

Part 1: Defining Market Drops 9

Part 2: Moving Averages 11

Part 3: The Green Line 17

Part 4: How to Enter the Trade 25

Part 5: How to Exit the Trade 29

Part 6: Summary of Strategy 35

Bonus Chapter: Market Crashes 37

Conclusion 41

Disclaimer

This book is written for informational, educational, and entertainment purposes only. By purchasing this book, you agree to NOT give any of the strategy presented in this book away in the review section of Amazon. Any reviews with information related to this strategy will be reported to Amazon and deleted.

The creator of this book is not an investment advisory service, a registered investment advisor, or a broker-dealer and does not advise clients on which securities they should buy or sell for themselves. It must be understood that a very high degree of risk is involved in trading stocks. The publisher of this book, and the affiliates of the publisher assume no responsibility or liability for trading and investment results. It should not be assumed that the methods, techniques, or indicators presented in this book will be profitable nor that they will not result in losses. In addition, the indicators, strategies, rules and all other features of the information presented are provided for information and educational purposes only and should not be construed as investment advice.

Investors and traders must always consult with their licensed financial advisors and tax advisors to determine the suitability of any investment. The author receives compensation for the affiliate links used in the book. The Green Line is trademarked® and copyrighted © 2020 with all rights reserved. Written by Tim Morris, published by ZML Corp LLC.

The Green Line

About the Author

Hello, my name is Tim Morris. I became known in the Kindle store with my first book related to finance titled *The Crash Signal*. Since then, I have continued coming out with new books to help traders profit in the market.

I have been trading and intensively studying the stock market for many years. You could say I'm somewhat obsessed, as I spend most of my free time reading and learning about stocks. Like most new traders, my initial attempt trading stocks was met with hardship and heartache. However, over the years through constant studying, I have come to have a much greater understanding of the stock market, and how to properly use it to build financial wealth.

My overall philosophy regarding the stock market is you can become wealthy investing in stocks when you focus on the *long-term*. Speculative strategies can be done, and definitely can be profitable, but they should not account for the majority of your portfolio. As such, while I have great faith in all my work, speculative strategies like the one laid out in this book should be performed with a small portion of your portfolio. My general rule is 90% long-term investing, 10% speculation.

If you have any questions while reading this book, feel free to email me at tim@trademorestocks.com. You can also find out more about me, other books I have written, and articles related to stocks on my website TradeMoreStocks.com.

NOTE: As stated in the disclaimer, please do not place any of this strategy in the review section of Amazon or you will be reported to Amazon and have your review deleted. Thank you.

Introduction

If you've done any research on stocks, you know there's a lot of promises out there. There's literally hundreds of "indicators" that supposedly tell you when to buy or sell stocks. There's so called gurus who claim to teach you their method, only to leave you high and dry when you buy their courses. Then there's the websites where you need to buy a monthly subscription, only to make mediocre gains or any at all. There's even "secret stock software" that supposedly has advanced algorithms to make you money. After all is said and done, there's a lot of promises out there, but unfortunately most of them don't deliver.

Like you, I've been through all this. I've bought the courses and books that were complete garbage and I would never want to put anyone through that. I think you will be very happy with this book and the strategy I am about to lay out for you. This strategy, which I have called *The Green Line*, involves an indicator which you can easily identify on your own without a subscription service or advanced software. One which you can use to make money when markets are down, getting you in close to the lowest point of the correction, which ends up providing you with the largest returns. This strategy takes the phrase "buy low, sell high" to a new level. Interested? Let's learn more about The Green Line.

The Green Line

Chapter 1
Defining Market Drops

First we'll go over the different types of drops that can occur in the stock market, in order to give you a better understanding of how this strategy works.

The first drop we'll go over is called a *dip*. These are small drops in the market, around 2%, that last a few days or weeks. On average, dips occur five times a year, and the market usually recovers fairly quickly from them.

The next drop we would call a *correction* and is the premise of this book. This is when the market drops 5%-20% from its highs. While corrections can take place rather rapidly, such as in The Flash Crash in 2010, usually they are more gradual. Corrections last longer than dips, taking place over a few weeks to a few months. On average, the stock market experiences one 14% market correction every year.

And the last type of drop is called a *crash*, which is synonymous with a bear market. This is when s*** hits the fan and people start crying. A crash is when the market drops over 20% from its highs. On average, there is a market crash every eight years.

In this book, we will be going over how to profit from *corrections*. I will teach you how to use the correction to your advantage by showing you an indicator that gets you in near the low, right when the market is about to recover. Depending on how much the market has dropped, this would mean an 8%-15% gain or more on your money in just a few weeks. Before we learn about The Green Line though, let's first go over moving averages, as well as the terminology you need to be aware of to use this strategy.

Chapter 2
Moving Averages

When referencing stock charts, there are indicators called moving averages, which you may already be familiar with. The most commonly touted moving average type is called the simple moving average (SMA). On charts, the SMA takes the average price of the last "X" number of periods, depending on what number you put in for X, and displays this average in the form of a line on a chart. The period is entered as a number, and calculated based on what timeframe interval you use. Here are definitions which explain this terminology in more detail:

- **Indicators** – Indicators are commonly used with technical analysis, and provide data to traders based on the price movement of a stock. Common indicators used by traders include moving average lines, the relative strength index, and stochastics.

- **Moving Average Type** – There are a variety of different *types* of moving averages, which differ in the formulas they use to display the moving average line on a chart. Some common moving average types include the simple moving average, exponential moving average, and triangular moving average.

- **Moving Average Period** – The moving average period, commonly called a lookback period, is a number you choose which tells the stock software how far to lookback to calculate the moving average line. The period is tied to the timeframe interval. For example, a 100 period SMA could look back 100 minutes, 100 days, 100 weeks, etc., depending on what timeframe interval was chosen.

- **Candlestick Chart** – A stock chart which uses candlesticks, as opposed to a line, to display the price action of a stock over a specified date range. The advantage to a candlestick chart, as opposed to a line chart, is the open, close, high, and low price of the specified timeframe interval is shown, as opposed to just the closing price with a line chart. The timeframe interval you choose for your candlestick chart determines the price action of each candlestick shown.

- **Timeframe Interval** – This is the price action of each "interval", for the timeframe you choose when viewing a chart. For example, if you were to pull up a stock chart with a "5 minute" timeframe interval, each candlestick in the chart shows you 5 minutes' worth of price action (open, close, high, low). If you were to instead choose a "weekly" timeframe interval, each candlestick shows you one week's worth of price action.

- **Date Range** – This is the total length of time the stock chart shows you. For example, if you pulled up a stock chart with a date range of 5 years, you'd see 5 years' worth of the stock price on your chart. Depending on what timeframe interval you chose (e.g. daily, weekly, etc.) would determine the candlesticks displayed on your chart over this entire date range.

Knowing all this terminology, we can now go over an example which will explain how moving averages are displayed on charts. Let's say we wanted to put a 20 period SMA line on a stock chart with a *daily* timeframe interval, which I'll call a daily chart. The charting software calculates the line by taking the closing price of the last 20 *days*, adding them all together, and then dividing them by 20 to show the average in the form of a line. This line is progressive, and continuously moves each day, as the price of said stock changes. It essentially smooths out the price for you, which allows you to use it as a reference point.

This 20 period SMA line would be different however, if placed on a *weekly* chart. This is because the SMA is now calculating the last 20 *weeks*, and showing you this average in the form of a line on the chart.

While simple moving averages are the most commonly mentioned moving averages by talking heads on TV, there is another type called the exponential moving average (EMA) which is not as widely mentioned. Like the SMA, the EMA averages the closing price of the last "X" number of periods, however it places more weight on the most recent periods. When charted, the EMA moves slightly higher or lower as compared to the SMA, depending on the direction the stock has moved more recently. This is significant for this strategy because with dips, corrections, and crashes, the most recent movements in the stock price are the most important. I have an example of this difference in the image on the next page, within a daily chart of ticker symbol AMD.

The Green Line

The Green Line I'm referring to in the book title is an EMA line with a specific lookback period placed onto a chart with a specific timeframe interval. And as I will show you, it has proved itself throughout history as a reliable support level during corrections. This EMA line is placed on one specific exchange traded fund (ETF), an ETF which correlates with the S&P 500.

The S&P 500 stands for the "Standards & Poor's 500 Index," which is a basket of the 500 largest publically traded companies in the United States. This index is commonly used by traders as a benchmark of the market. As in, it's referenced by traders to determine how the stock market as a whole is doing. This is because many stocks, whether inside or outside the S&P 500, usually follow the same path. As in, if the S&P

500 is up or down big on the day, week, month, etc., many stocks in the market also follow this same trend. When listening to financial broadcasts or the talking heads on TV say something like, "the market is up 100 points today," they are usually referring to the S&P 500.

Exchange traded funds, commonly abbreviated as ETFs, are a basket of individual stocks, combined into one ticker symbol. What this does is allow investors to have a large number of stocks in their portfolio without having to buy each stock individually. At the same time, it can make diversifying much easier. This is because many ETFs are available which include a variety of different companies within different sectors.

The most common ETF which correlates with the S&P 500 is called the "SPDR S&P 500 Trust," with ticker symbol SPY. When you buy this ETF, you are essentially buying the entire S&P 500. However, instead of having to buy all 500 stocks in the S&P 500, you can just buy this one ticker symbol, which includes all 500 stocks for you.

The Green Line

As **a token of appreciation** to my readers, I am offering my special report titled *Crush the Market* **absolutely free!** In this report, you will learn 14 incredibly beneficial tips which will help you make money in the stock market. Just copy & paste the link below into your browser and put in your email address, and it will immediately be sent to you!

linkpony.com/crush

Chapter 3
The Green Line

History repeats itself. Historians repeat each other.
- Philip Guedalla

History is a reliable indicator of what will happen in the future, and this is especially true in the stock market. Based on what history has shown there is one EMA period and chart timeframe which, combined together, have served as a reliable indicator at predicting the bottom of market corrections, specifically on the S&P 500 index. Considering this, we will be using the exchange traded fund SPY, an ETF which mirrors the S&P 500, as the main chart we focus on in this book.

The EMA line and timeframe I'm about to refer to act as a net, causing SPY to bounce off of it. I say a net and not a wall because sometimes it will bounce a little before the net, sometimes a little after the net, and sometimes right at the net, but all in all history has shown SPY commonly bounces off this net during stock market corrections.

As I've explained, there are many different periods and timeframes you can reference when viewing a moving average line on a stock chart. So what exactly am I referring to here?

The Green Line

The Green Line I'm referring to in the book title is the *50 period EMA line*, displayed in a *weekly* timeframe interval on a stock chart. The reason I named this book The Green Line, is because I make this line green in my stock charting software, so the name just kind of stuck.

I will be using the words *The Green Line* and *50 EMA* interchangeably throughout the rest of this book, as you now know they mean the same thing.

The easiest way I have found to view the 50 EMA on a weekly chart is to use the website Yahoo Finance. As a courtesy, I'm providing a shortened link for your reference. Just go to linkpony.com/spy. This will bring you right to the Yahoo Finance chart for SPY. Once there, you'll want to choose an interval of "1 Week" in the upper tool bar. Then click the "indicator" button in the top left, and choose "moving average." Here, you will change the period to 50, and then change the type of moving average to "exponential." You will now have a 50 period EMA displayed on a weekly chart of SPY for you to reference for this strategy.

As stated previously, the market typically incurs a 14% correction every year. This statistic is just an average though, and that's important to remember. Corrections range from 5%-20% and can sometimes occur multiple times in the same year, and other times not occur at all in a year. Regardless of these variances though, The Green Line has maintained itself as a reliable support level during corrections.

Using the ETF SPY, let's go over some examples of how the 50 EMA has proved itself through recent history. The ETF SPY was created in 1993, thus making the 50 EMA line not available until mid-1994. This is when our examples will start.

From 1995 to 1999, there were a total of 6 corrections. During all of these corrections, SPY came down to touch its 50 EMA, bounced, and then proceeded to ascend past its former high each time. Had you bought at the 50 EMA, you could have capitalized on all 6 of these corrections over this 5 year period.

Then, early in the year 2000, the famous dot com crash occurred, which caused the market to drop nearly 50% from its highs. As you're aware, The Green Line is only meant to be used during stock market corrections, *not* during crashes. As such, we would not have used this strategy during this time period. You may be thinking, how would you know a crash was going to occur, as opposed to just another correction? We will cover this in the subsequent chapters.

The Green Line

The stock market regained composure in 2003 and started moving higher. From 2003 – 2006, a total of five corrections occurred over this four year period. During each correction, The Green Line again served as a valid support level, allowing you to enter near the bottom, before the market regained its former high.

In 2007, a financial crisis occurred in the banking sector, causing a stock market crash. During this crash, the S&P 500 dropped over 50% from its high before regaining composure in 2011, which is where our next example begins.

From 2011 to 2019, a total of nine stock market corrections occurred over this nine year period.

Tim Morris

21

The Green Line

When looking at the chart on the previous page, you may notice two rather large corrections occurred in 2016 and 2018, which moved well past the 50 EMA line. I have them shown in the image below.

While rare, as it only has occurred two times over the last 30 years, larger corrections are something that need to be discussed. These need not make you worry though, as I have found the *200 EMA* line, again referenced on a weekly chart, served as an additional support level when these larger corrections occurred. During the two larger corrections, occurring in 2016 and 2018, SPY descended past its 50 EMA, touched its 200 EMA, and then bounced higher.

The additional line shown in the picture above is the 200 EMA. In the next chapter, we will go over how to enter and exit the 50 EMA during a correction, as well as what to do if SPY drops to its 200 EMA.

The Green Line

Chapter 4
How to Enter the Trade

As explained in the previous chapter, during a correction SPY usually drops to its 50 EMA, before bouncing from it and moving higher. However there are rare times when it will instead go through the 50 EMA, and continue down to the 200 EMA before bouncing higher. And then there are even rarer times when the market descends below the 200 EMA and a market crash occurs. How should we handle these situations?

The first thing we need to go over is how to anticipate that a crash may be occurring, as opposed to just a correction. While obviously a crash is more rare, you still wouldn't want to get caught in one if just planning for a correction. In my book *The Crash Signal*, I provide a signal that has predicted every stock market crash since World War II. So if the market begins declining and you see SPY descending towards its 50 EMA, the first thing you should do is check to see if The Crash Signal has flashed. If it hasn't, this trade becomes much safer to enter as it's more likely we're just experiencing a correction.

While you could technically buy *any* stock when SPY touches The Green Line, not all stocks follow the market exactly. A much more reliable way to perform this trade would be to actually buy SPY, or a 2x or 3x leveraged ETF which also correlate with the S&P

500. As such, here are the ticker symbols I would recommend using for this trade, moving from the lowest to highest risk level:

SPY
S&P 500 non-leveraged ETF

SSO
S&P 500 2x leveraged ETF

UPRO
S&P 500 3x leveraged ETF

For those unfamiliar, a leveraged ETF is in essence a multiplier. For example, let's take UPRO, the 3x leveraged S&P 500 ETF. If SPY moved *up* 1% on a given day, UPRO would move up 3% on that same day. However with more potential reward comes more potential risk. This means if SPY moved *down* by 1% on a given day, UPRO would move down 3% on that same day. For this reason, if you are unfamiliar with leveraged ETFs or don't have money to risk, stay away from them!

If you decide to trade SSO or UPRO, use SPY's chart touching The Green Line as a guide of when to buy. Don't set up the 50 EMA on SSO or UPRO itself.

Before you enter this trade, you must first determine the amount you want to allocate towards it. While we will be putting a stop-loss in place, meaning your risk will be lowered, you still don't want to risk money you can't afford to lose. Ultimately trading in the stock market is gambling, and while the odds will be in your favor with this trade, it's still possible to lose money. For this reason, you aren't taking out a new mortgage or selling your car to finance this trade. Only use money which isn't going to hinder your life if you happened to lose some of it. For example, when I have performed this trade in the past, I used the cash equivalent of 5% of my overall portfolio to finance it. This is just an example and your level of risk may be different from mine.

Most of the time SPY will bounce off The Green Line and continue higher. However, as mentioned before, in rare occasions it will continue descending to its 200 EMA. For this reason, after you allocate how much you want to spend on this trade, I would suggest splitting your funds into thirds. Two/thirds of your funds will be used to buy SPY once it touches its 50 EMA. Then, if SPY continues to descend downward, you will use the remaining one/third of your funds to purchase SPY should it touch its 200 EMA. Splitting your funds up like this allows you to cost average into the trade, which equates to a larger profit potential.

While a correction is inevitable in the stock market, how each correction retraces after touching The Green Line has proved to be unique. During some corrections, SPY bounces right off The Green Line and immediately moves back to its prior highs within just a few days. Other times, weeks can go by before SPY regains its prior highs. The point here is you need to have a limit order in place *before* SPY touches its 50 EMA. So pay attention to the market. Once you see SPY descending on its chart, put in your limit order at its 50 EMA.

Having a limit order in place beforehand allows you to capitalize on this trade, should SPY bounce off its 50 EMA and then quickly retrace higher. Sometimes SPY has bounced very quickly, even within just one day. Considering you're unlikely to be on your phone all day checking the markets, having that limit order in place beforehand keeps you from missing the trade and crying all night should a quick bounce occur. Let's go over an example.

You've noticed the market has been down the last few days or weeks, and SPY is beginning to descend towards The Green Line. You would place a limit order at the 50 EMA using 2/3 of your allotted funds and then wait. Monitor your position each day, and move your limit order up or down accordingly, as the 50 EMA line can move slightly each day as the price of SPY changes.

After your order is triggered, you will continue monitoring your position by checking SPY each day. You want to have both the 50 EMA and 200 EMA set up on your chart because if SPY continues descending, the 200 EMA is the next place it will go. As discussed previously, it most likely *will not* go down to the 200 EMA, but it is possible.

In the first case scenario, your limit-order at the 50 EMA is triggered. It may bounce around or move slightly lower, but it *does not* continue descending to the 200 EMA. SPY then starts moving higher in the coming days and weeks. We will go over our exit strategy in the next chapter.

In the second scenario, your 1st limit order is triggered at the 50 EMA line, but then SPY continues descending and starts to approach its 200 EMA. Here you'd put in your 2nd limit order with the remaining 1/3 of your allocated funds at the 200 EMA line. Just like before, you will monitor this limit order and move it up or down accordingly each day so it remains positioned on the 200 EMA line. When your limit order is executed, immediately put in a stop-loss order 10% below the 200 EMA. While it's highly unlikely to touch your stop-loss, this safety precaution will be put into place to protect your money in the unlikely event of a market crash.

Chapter 5
How to Exit the Trade

Okay, your limit order has executed and the market is starting to ascend higher. How should you get out? What I've found is a good place to exit this position is the *previous high* the market had made. This is because sometimes things can get wobbly here, and it might take a little bit of time before it breaks this high again. Considering you're most likely just performing this trade to make a little extra cash and SPY isn't in your full time portfolio, you want to make the largest amount of profit in the shortest amount of time.

Let's go over three examples of exiting this trade from different years.

The Green Line

This first example is from 1997, where SPY just corrects to the 50 EMA.

Here, SPY made a high of $98.50 in the second week of October before the market correction started. Over the coming three weeks, SPY started trending lower, touching its 50 EMA at the end of October at a price of $85.29. After touching its 50 EMA, SPY briefly moved lower for just one day, but then soared higher. Over the next five weeks, SPY continued moving higher and finally came back to its previous high of $98.50 in the first week of December. This resulted in a gain of $13.21 per share. As discussed previously, there are three ETFs which could be traded during these corrections. Here are the profit profiles based on which ETF was chosen to trade:

SPY - 15.49% Profit   **SSO** - 30.98% Profit   **UPRO** - 46.47% Profit

The next chart is from 2012, where again SPY just corrects to The Green Line.

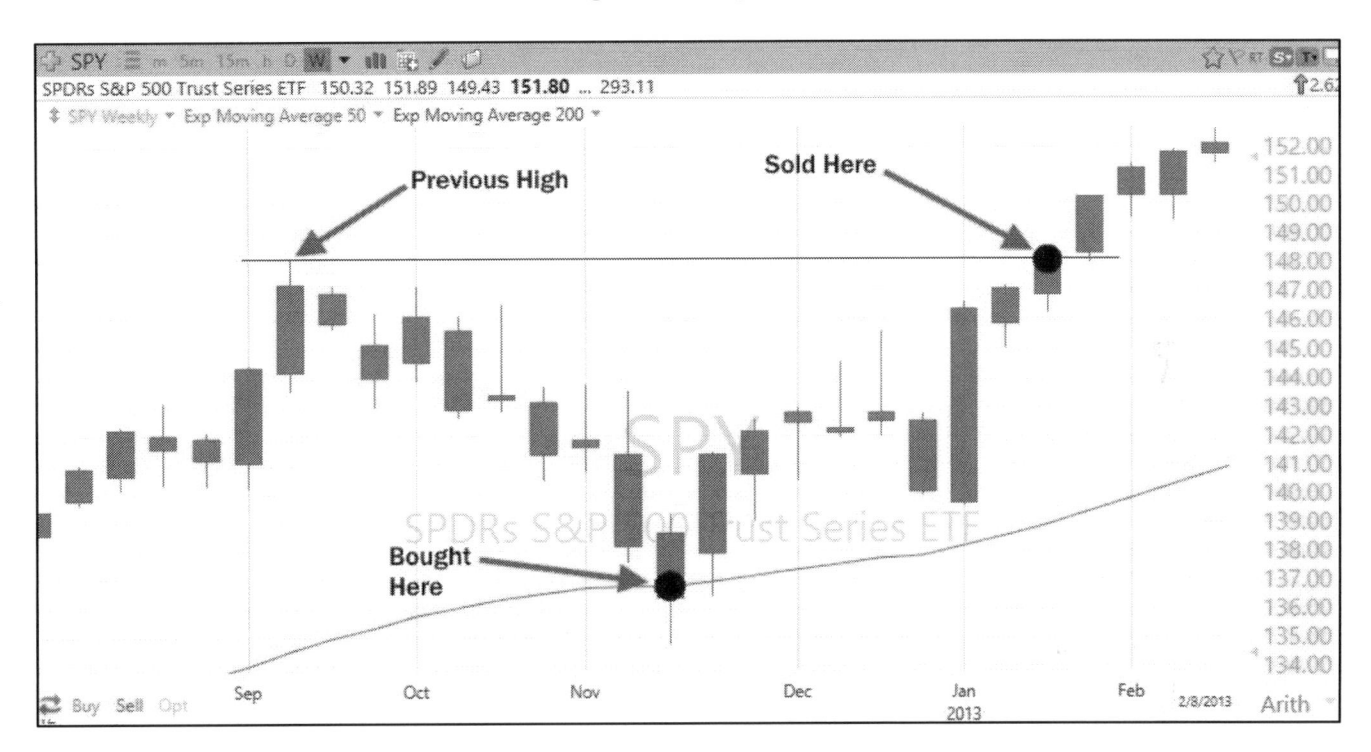

In the 2nd week of September, SPY reached a high of $148.11 before the market started its correction. Over the next nine weeks SPY descended lower, touching its 50 EMA in the third week of November at a price of $136.71. After touching its 50 EMA, SPY briefly moved lower for just two days, before regaining composure and making its ascent higher. Nine weeks later, in the third week of January 2013, the market regained its previous high of $148.11. This comes out to a gain of $11.40 per share. Here are the profit profiles based on which ETF was chosen to trade:

SPY – 8.34% Profit   **SSO** – 16.68% Profit   **UPRO** – 25.02% Profit

The Green Line

Let's go over one more example, except this time we will include the 200 EMA. This example is from the correction which occurred at the end of 2018.

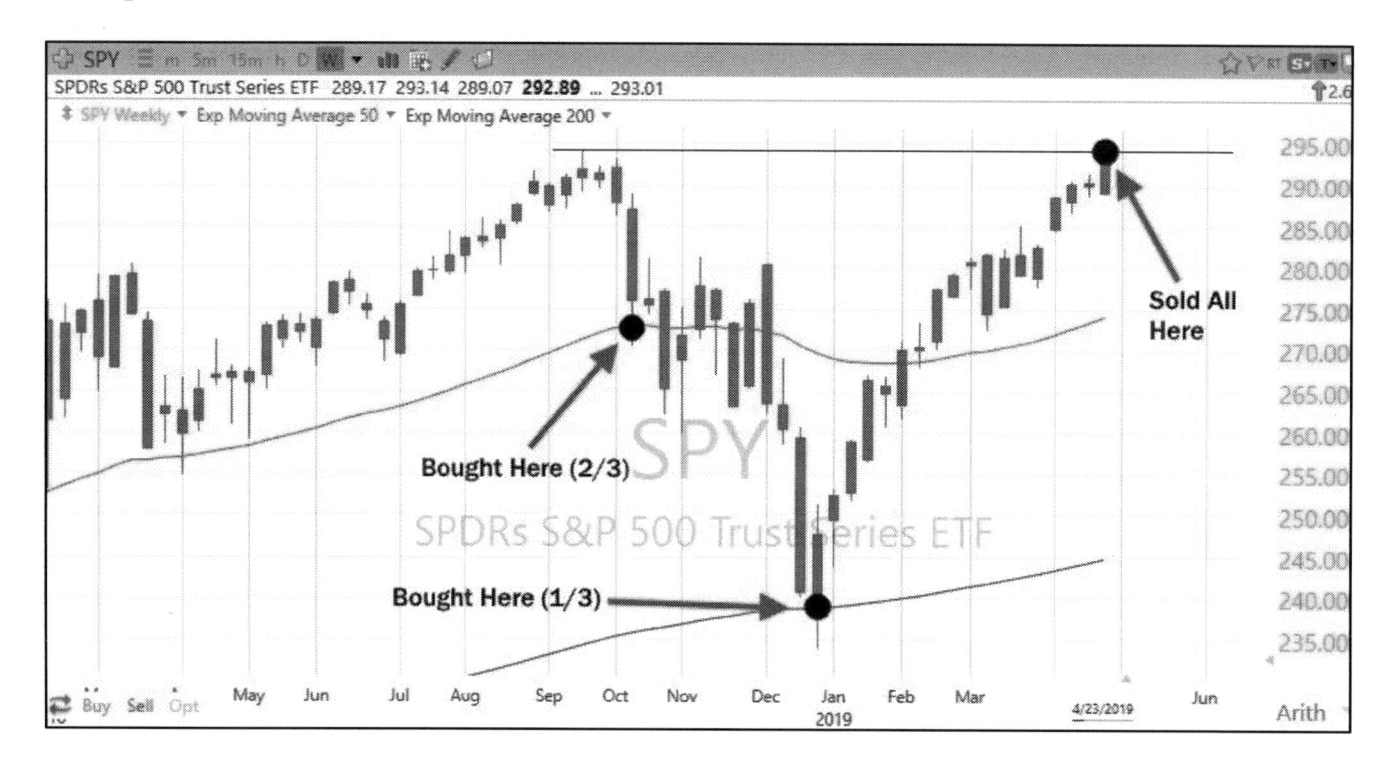

In the third week of September, SPY made a high of $293.94 before the market's correction started. In just one week, SPY fell to its 50 EMA line at a price of $272.77. At this point, our limit order with 2/3 of our allotted funds would have been executed.

Over the next ten weeks, SPY bounced wildly around its 50 EMA line, before dropping lower in the last week of December. SPY then touched its 200 EMA at a price of $238.74, at which point our second limit order using the remaining 1/3 of our allotted funds would have been executed. We would then have placed a stop-loss 10% lower than our entry point, at a price of $214.86.

After touching its 200 EMA, SPY moved lower for just one day before quickly propelling higher. It took 17 weeks, or around 4 months, but SPY regained its high of $293.94 and our position would have been sold. Our dollar cost average was $261.44, meaning a gain of $32.50 per share.

This resulted in the following profit profiles, based on which ETF was chosen to trade:

SPY – 12.83% Profit   **SSO** – 25.66% Profit   **UPRO** – 38.49% Profit

Customer Reviews

⭐⭐⭐⭐⭐ 38

4.8 out of 5 stars ▼

5 star	▅▅▅▅▅	87%
4 star	▏	10%
3 star		3%
2 star		0%
1 star		0%

See all 38 customer reviews ▸

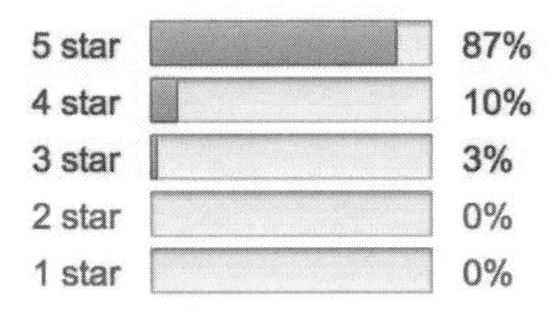

Share your thoughts with other customers

[Write a customer review]

If you are enjoying this book, could you please leave a review on Amazon? It would be greatly appreciated and allow me to come out with more informative books in the future. A shortened link to the review page is below:

linkpony.com/green

Chapter 6
Summary of Strategy

Here's a summary of how to execute this trade:

1. You notice the market has been declining. Bring up a *weekly* chart of SPY on Yahoo Finance, and add the 50 EMA and 200 EMA into the chart.

2. Check for The Crash Signal (TCS).
   a. If TCS has flashed, do not perform this trade, as there is a high likelihood the "correction" could actually be the beginning of a bear market.
   b. If TCS has not flashed, move to step 3.

3. Determine the amount of funds you will allocate towards the trade.
   a. Place a limit order at the 50 EMA using 2/3 of your allocated funds.
   b. If the market moves lower, place a limit order at the 200 EMA on the same weekly chart, using the remaining 1/3 of your funds.
   c. Put a stop-loss in place *only* if your 2nd limit order at the 200

35

EMA is executed. The stop-loss should be 10% below the 200 EMA line. If only the first limit order is executed at the 50 EMA line, do not put in a stop-loss.

4. Use the market's previous high as an exit point.

By using all four steps to this strategy, you now have a high probability trade which you can use to make consistent profits during stock market corrections.

Something else I want to mention is SPY may hit The Green Line during pre-market or after-market hours. For this reason, make sure the limit order you enter has the ability to execute *outside* of normal market hours.

To do this, brokers usually require you to click a checkbox when entering your limit order, which tells them you are allowing the trade to be executed outside normal market hours. As such, make sure you click this checkbox when entering your order.

Bonus Chapter
Market Crashes

While preparing this book I noticed something interesting which I wanted to bring up in this bonus chapter. What I found was while The Green Line is a reliable support level during a market correction, it also becomes a reliable *resistance* level during a market crash. This would mean during the small rallies that occur within bear markets, The Green Line essentially becomes the top before the market continues its move lower.

In order to profit from a declining stock price during a market crash, you normally would have to "short" the stock. Luckily, there are "inverse ETFs" which make this process much easier than taking out short positions on the S&P 500. These inverse ETFs go up when the S&P 500 goes down. And just like the ETFs mentioned in chapter four, there are non-leveraged and leveraged versions of these inverse ETFs as well. These inverse ETFs can be bought with your broker, just like you would buy any regular stock symbol. The three inverse ETFs which correlate with the S&P 500 are:

SH - S&P 500 non-leveraged inverse ETF

SDS - S&P 500 2x leveraged inverse ETF

SPXU - S&P 500 3x leveraged inverse ETF

The Green Line

Let's go over two examples where The Green Line acted as resistance during a market crash. The first example will be from the market crash of 2000, and the second example will be from the market crash of 2008.

2000 Market Crash

In March of the year 2000, SPY made a high of $155.75. Over the next two years, a bear market ensued, where the S&P 500 dropped in value by almost 50%. It reached a low in October of 2002, at a price of $78.20. However during it's descent, the market had small rallies in which it moved up to touch its 50 EMA line a total of four times. Each time SPY touched The Green Line, it quickly descended below its previous low within a few weeks.

2008 Market Crash

In October of 2007, SPY made a high of $157.52. Over the next two years, a bear market ensued, which pushed the S&P 500 down to a low of $67.10, a 57% decline. During this two year period, SPY came back to touch its 50 EMA line once. And again, just like the previous crash, The Green Line acted as a resistance level in which the market bounced and moved downward, past its previous low.

We would use the same process of entering and exiting our position as mentioned in chapter six of this book, just in an inverse fashion. So during a crash, if SPY were to come up and touch The Green Line, we would buy one of the inverse ETFs just mentioned. Then when SPY moved back down and touched its previous low point, we would have a limit order in place to sell our position.

There are two slight differences I would recommend though with this bear market strategy. The first difference would be to only use the 50 EMA and *not* the 200 EMA. As such, you wouldn't split your allotted funds into thirds, but instead just buy the inverse ETF at the 50 EMA with the full amount you allocate towards the trade.

The second difference would be placing a stop-loss 5% above your entry point. This is because the market typically does not move much higher than The Green Line during a crash, and if it does, it most likely means the crash is ending. We would want to have a safety measure in place should the market continue to ascend higher.

While this is a fairly safe bear market trade in itself, there is a way to provide an additional layer of protection for your money. Before entering the trade, you can check for a signal known as "The Golden Cross." The Golden Cross is an indicator followed by many traders which signals that a market crash is effectively over, and a recovery has started. This golden cross occurs when the 50 period simple moving average crosses above the 200 period simple moving average displayed on a chart of SPY within a *daily* timeframe. Meaning each candlestick on this chart would represent one day's worth of price action, as opposed to the weekly timeframe interval we've used throughout the book.

In summary, during a bear market you'd first check for a golden cross on a chart of SPY within a daily timeframe. If the cross has not occurred, you can then follow the strategy I just went over, which will allow you to capitalize on the small rallies which are very typical during bear markets.

Conclusion

I hope you enjoyed this book and learned a useful strategy that will help you generate income during market corrections. Feel free to email me with any questions you have at tim@trademorestocks.com.

Also, you can find more stock tips on my website TradeMoreStocks.com. I wish you the best in your financial endeavors!

If you enjoyed this book, you may also like:

TIM MORRIS　　　　　　　　　　　　　　　　TRADEMORESTOCKS.COM

ONE-ON-ONE STOCK COACHING

Get the Help You Need to Make Long Term Profits in the Market!

Shortened Link to Webpage:
linkpony.com/coach

Need a little help with your portfolio? Tim has you covered! By signing up for a coaching session, Tim will sit down with you for a one hour phone call, where he lays out a customized plan for you to start generating income in the markets.

Tim explains how the markets operates, the best portfolio allocation, and the reasons why the long term strategy he will go over with you works so well. When you're finished talking, you'll have a better understanding of the stock market and a defined plan for your financial future. Find out more at the link above now!

The 20% Solution

A Long Term Investment Strategy that Averages 20.13% Per Year

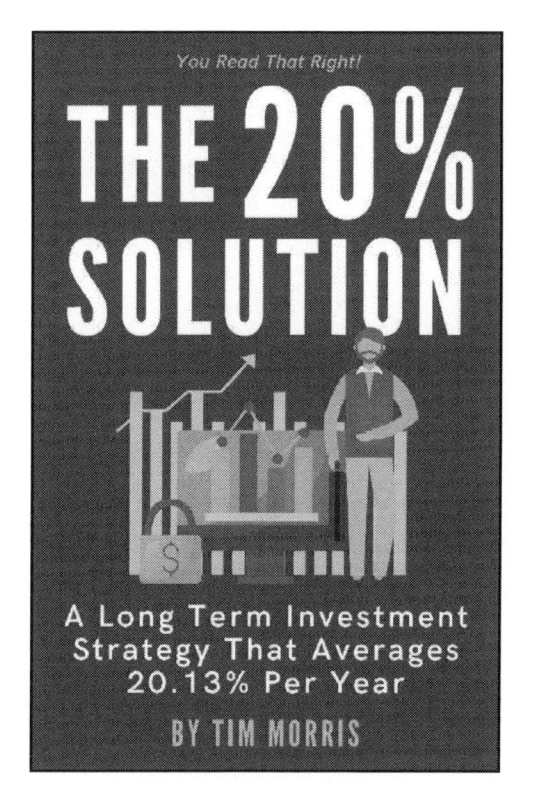

Shortened Link to Book:
linkpony.com/20

You read that right, 20.13% per year! This strategy, which I have coined *The 20% Solution*, requires just 4 trades a year. And of those 4 trades, very little is destined to capital gains tax. This book includes 30 years of history of this strategy in action, with charts and figures to back it up. Go to the link above to find out more!

The Crash Signal
The One Signal that Predicts a Stock Market Crash

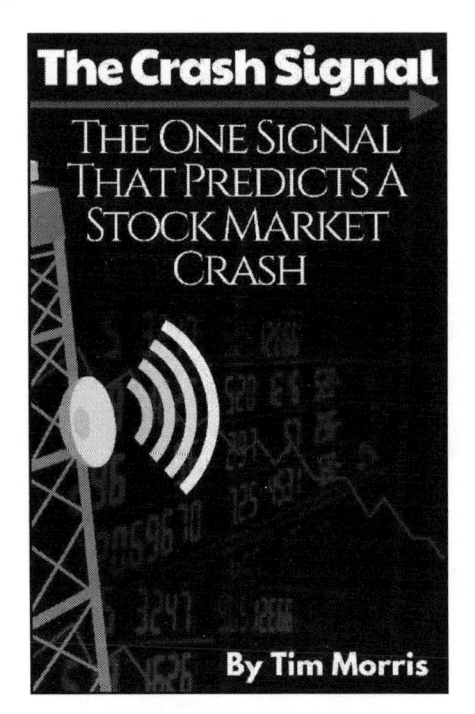

Shortened Link to Book:
linkpony.com/crash

Stock market crashes are inevitable, but losing money doesn't have to be! In this ground breaking book, Tim Morris exposes the one signal that has flashed before every stock market crash for the last 60 years. He then tells you the exact point to get out to avoid the crash, & even how to make money while it's happening! Save yourself from the next crash with The Crash Signal!

Made in the USA
Monee, IL
22 November 2020